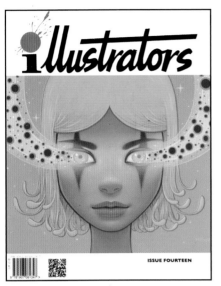

Cover Image: Tara McPherson

Illustrators

The Book Palace
Jubilee House
Bedwardine Road
Crystal Palace
London SE19 3AP
Email: IQ@bookpalace.com
Web: www.bookpalace.com
Contact GW: gw@bookpalace.com
Tel: 020 8768 0022
(From overseas +44 20 8768 0022)
Publisher: Geoff West
Editor & Designer: Peter Richardson
Layouts Tara McPherson, Joe Jusko - Diego Cordoba
Consultant Editor: David Ashford
Featured Writers: Peter Richardson, Diego Cordoba, Brooke Boynton Hughes
Website: Paul Tanner
Subscriptions & Distribution: David Howarth
Advertising: IQ@bookpalace.com

illustrators ISBN 978-1-907081-34-7
ISSN 2052-6520
Issue Number Fourteen Published Spring 2016
Copyright © 2016 by The Book Palace Ltd.
All text and artwork copyright is vested with the respective creators and publishers. None of the material within these pages may be reproduced without the written consent of *illustrators* or the aforementioned copyright holders. The images reproduced within these pages are for research purposes and all efforts have been made to ensure their historical accuracy.

illustrators is published quarterly.
Each issue £18 Post FREE worldwide
UK £49 for 4 issues including 4 FREE digital issues
EU/USA £66 for 4 issues including 4 FREE digital issues
ROW £72 for 4 issues including 4 FREE digital issues

Available in the USA from **budplant.com**
Trade Orders: IQ@bookpalace.com

Printed in China by Prolong Press Ltd

CONTENTS

EDITORIAL

Tara McPherson's iconography is instantly recognizable—water, space and heart-shaped cavities surround and shape her characters, who wander through their universe with an aura of elegant detachment. Her paintings command your attention and colour your dreams. She has an international following and a work ethic to match. Diego Cordoba has been finding out more about this remarkable artist and her evolution.

Diego Cordoba returns, as he shares with us the work of one of the most precociously talented artists (he sold his first artwork to *Heavy Metal* magazine at the tender age of 17!) currently on the scene. Joe Jusko's work has dominated the superhero scene for much of the last three decades and his story is every bit as inspirational as the art that he creates.

Maurice Leloir's illustrations brought to life the world of 17th century France: an age of romance, swordplay and excess. As David Ashford reveals, he was responsible for the first illustrated edition of Alexandre Dumas' 'The Three Musketeers' and his talent commanded the attention of Douglas Fairbanks for his cinematic adaptation of Dumas' 'The Man in the Iron Mask'.

Adam Stower's work is steeped in the traditional skills of superb draftsmanship, exquisite storytelling and a love of the craft of illustration. His warm and engaging personality has seen him travel the world, bringing his stories to life for children from Durham to Geneva, from Cape Town to the Caribbean. We talk to him about his career and his art in another of our regular interviews.

Mike Zagorski is a total one-off. Thanks to Ron Murphy (see issue 12) we were able to check out Mike's feet-first artwork—we were knocked out and I am sure you will be too.

Lastly, we thought we would reintroduce you to one of the stars from issue 3. Fortunino Matania's artwork is something you can never get enough of.

The opinions expressed in *illustrators* are those of the writers, and are not necessarily those of the editor and publishers. The accuracy of the authentication of all images is the responsibility of the contributors.

Tara McPherson

Discover the sweet and strange surreal world of this multifaceted artist as Diego Cordoba tells us about her love for Japanese art, mysticism and astronomy

ABOVE: *Dark Matter Witch* (2010), oil and silver leaf on linen, stretched over panel, 15" x 30", part of the *Bunny in the Moon* series.

RIGHT: *Bunny in the Moon* (2010), oil on linen, stretched over panel, 40" x 30". The title comes from a Japanese legend about a bunny that sacrificed his life to feed a starving man that was actually a deity in disguise. In homage to the selflessness the bunny showed, the deity made his ashes fly to the moon so all could remember his kind act and his image for ages to come.

THE PAINTINGS OF TARA MCPHERSON convey a certain sweetness with their pastel-like colours (though mostly done with oils), combined with an outer-world strangeness that adds to their surrealistic power. Often described as 'creepy' (for lack of a better understanding) there is, in fact, nothing ugly nor anything to fear about her paintings. It may be owing to the uneasiness they might generate, or their apparent darkness, that has led fans and critics to call them 'creepy'. But far from it, Tara's paintings are a world on their own, ethereal and beautiful, and seem more influenced by Japanese art (particularly Hokusai, Hiroshigi, Yoshitoshi, and Kuniyoshi prints, manga and anime) than by Western art, which might lead people to think of her work as 'weird'.

"It's partly due to my interest in modern Japanese art," she once said. "I love the way it depicts monsters, but also these cute, sweet girls who are really badass. I've always liked depicting strong women. It's a really fun balance—if I do something that's all sweet, I feel it has no edge and there's something missing."

Her attraction to the human figure has also led her to look closely at the Renaissance masters' Mannerist paintings, notably the work of 16th century artist Agnolo di Cosimo, better known as Bronzino, whose skin-tones Tara admires, and the way Klimt merged Japanese and Western

ABOVE: *The Death of Boto* (2010), oil on linen, stretched over panel, 35" x 48". Based on the pink-tinged fresh-water river dolphin, also known as the *Boto Encantado*, a shape-shifting, maiden-wooing, wave-surfing romancer of the jungle river villages of Amazonia. BELOW: *Inertia* (2013), oil on wood panel, 30" x 30", from *Wandering Luminations*.

BELOW: *The Love Space Gives Is as Deep as the Oceans* (2010), oil on linen, stretched over panel, 45" x 48", from the *Bunny in the Moon* cycle, and featuring one of Tara's goth-like female characters with a hole in her chest in the shape of a heart.

lore. Though Tara's paintings are mostly figurative. There are three main elements that are recurring factors in most of her work: the first is water, as an element of life, be it as rain, waterfalls, sea or lakes. In Tara's hands, this water might glow with a phosphorescent luminescence, as though coming from an underworld, but somehow surging with life too. The second element is space, empty space that surrounds us in the universe, sometimes with a cluster of constellations, sometimes on its own: empty, remote, and bringing forth a sense of loneliness. The third element comprises her female characters, often with a hole in the chest in the shape of a heart, as if telling us that they are heartless entities caught in a void, or have just gone through

LEFT: *Bunny Girl* (2010), oil on linen, stretched over panel, 18" x 24", from the *Bunny in the Moon* series.
BELOW: *Sometimes I Just Want a Hug* (2005), acrylic, 12" x 26", done for the 'Sometimes I want a Hug' group exhibition at the Jonathan Levine gallery in NYC.

a heartbreak and can't express their love anymore. Yet they aren't desperate and suicidal figures filled with anguish, but rather the contrary: they seem at peace, though devoid of emotion, bringing a somehow mysterious and serene tranquillity to the whole setting. As to the origin of the character with the cut-out heart (since named Orion), Tara says:

"Well, originally, I went through a really horrible break-up, and I painted the very first one. It just helped me get through a very rough time emotionally, and really get out what I needed to get out. It was very cathartic. That's initially how she started.

"And then I just really liked the character, in and of itself. With seeing

Text continues on page 9

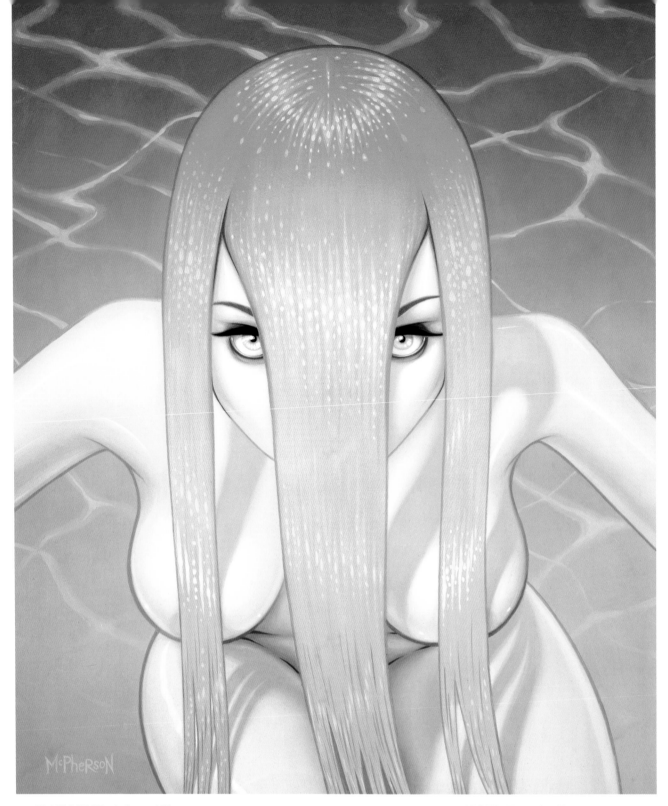

FACING PAGE: *Safety of Water*
(2010), oil on linen, stretched over
panel, 60" x 48", based on a myth
that originates from an ancient
Greek didactic text, the *Epiphanius*,
where the elephants ready to give
birth would find safety from their
enemies by entering a small body
of water. The Kappa riding him,
having a pool of water on his head,
freezes if the water spills.

ABOVE: *From the Abyss*
(2009), oil on birch, 20" x 24",
from the *Fractal Lake* series.
A stunning painting where we
can see the influence
of Japanese folklore,
especially from the ghost
story legend of the black hair,
famed in the film *Kwaidan* and
the books of
Lafcadio Hearn.

Text continued from page 5

experiences that friends go through in life, in their relationships and friendships, I was able to funnel that emotion into my work. We all experience these basic deep human emotions at times, this feeling of loss, whether it's love or death. Sometimes it can be difficult to verbalize, but everyone experiences it. So this character is able to encompasses that visually. I really enjoy that image."

Add to these the ethereal settings, flowers with eyeballs, strange but cute three-eyed small animals, and black, blob-like amorphous creatures (based on the sea-spirit of Japanese folklore known as the Umibōzu), accompanied by the often Gothic-like human figures, and you start getting an idea of what Tara's world is all about.

Although she's worked with lots of different media, she has been using mostly oils for the past 10 years. Each painting is a labour of love, taking her weeks (or months) to accomplish in usually a large size and in a very polished, almost digital   -looking, way, though it's all done by hand with brushes and paint. "My work is definitely not of this world. It's very illustrative, surreal and dreamlike, and I'm interested in pop culture, so the term 'pop surrealist' really encompasses what I'm doing. Some people talk about 'lowbrow art', but I don't like that term. My work isn't 'low' anything."

In recent years Tara's paintings also follow a similarly thematic cycle, which continually evolves and changes into the next cycle, offering us a chance not only to see how this extraordinary artist develops creatively,

FACING PAGE: *Laughing Through The Chaos Of It All* (2008), oil, 20" x 24", part of the *Fractal Lake* cycle, featuring two components of Tara's art, the balloon-like *Wiggles* and the girl with the heart-shaped hollow chest.
ABOVE LEFT: *Playing With Fire-The Healer* (2009), oil on birch, 20" x 30".
ABOVE RIGHT: *Playing With Fire-The Handler* (2009), oil on birch, 24" x 30", also from the *Fractal Lake* series.

Text continues on page 16

ABOVE: *Electric Lola* (2015), oil on birch, 18" x 18", part of the *I Know It By Heart* series, with a Lolita-like nymph and a cosmic explosion around her.

FACING PAGE: *Quantum Dancer* (2015), oil on birch, 30" x 36", part of the *I Know It By Heart* series, which carries on Tara's exploration of ethereal imagery with portraits of young girls caught in a magical out-of-this-world moment.

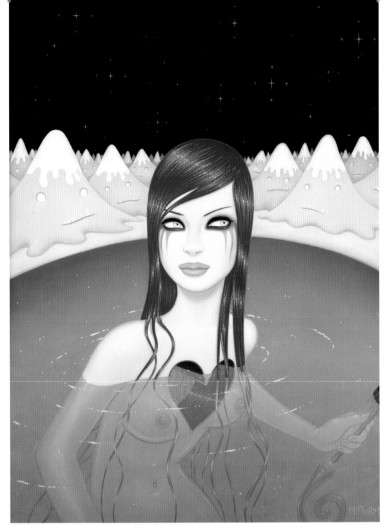

PREVIOUS PAGES SPREAD LEFT: *Evolution of Language* (2008), oil, 20" x 30", part of the *Lost Constellations* series, where we see Tara's trademark of a hollow-chested girl with *Wiggle* balloons.

PREVIOUS PAGES SPREAD RIGHT: *Magnetic Destroyer* (2015), oil on panel, 18" x 24" from the *I Know It By Heart* series where "the paintings ended up taking an adventure towards visual manifestations, literally things coming out of their eyes, with aurora, rays of viruses. smoke, water, electricity, or even a lack of visual contact with eyes covered or a glance away from the viewer."

FACING PAGE: *Lost Constellations* (2008), oil and acrylic on birch, 30" x 40", featuring one of the truly "creepy" paintings attributed to Tara.

ABOVE LEFT: *The Weight Of Water, Part One* (2008), oil, 30" x 40" from the *Lost Constellations* series where "A donut umbrella will never line up with the eye of the storm."

ABOVE RIGHT: *The Weight Of Water, Part Two* (2008), oil, 30" x 40". "The planet has cried and now I'm swimming in a pool of tears."

LEFT: *The Weight Of Water, Part Three* (2008), oil, 30" x 40". "I've always dreamt of being naked and frozen on another planet."

15

Text continued from page 9

ABOVE: *The Silent Hero* (2009), oil on linen, 24" x 20", this painting is about how silence and the inability to speak can be a virtue in life sometimes. From the 'Silent Heroes' exhibition at Iguapop Gallery in Barcelona, Spain held on July 9th, 2009. **FACING PAGE TOP:** *Untitled I* (2009), pencil, India ink and acrylic on Arches watercolor paper for the same exhibition.

but what new ideas come from her colourful mind.

As to her working process, she usually starts a piece by doing some writing and little roughs. "Writing and brainstorming to get my ideas out is always my initial approach, no matter what, whether it's a fine art painting for a gallery show, a rock poster or an illustration. The writing helps me solidify the concept and the direction I want to go in. You can make some interesting connections if you're just brainstorming and throwing words out there… kind of getting a flow of consciousness."

Then she does small-sized roughs: if it works at a small size, she knows it will work on the board or canvas, whatever size she blows it up to. "It is really hard for me to start initially using a 14 by 17 sheet of paper: it's too big. So, I do tiny roughs and then develop it from there. Then I scan the rough drawings, enlarge them, choose a layout and put it on the light table where I do my main drawing. There's something captured in that fluidity and looseness in the roughness—if

I try to re-draw it by eye, it gets very stiff. So I loosely trace out my rough on to the drawing paper so I get that gestural quality and freeness that was there in the tiny drawing".

If it's a painting, she will stop there and transfer it to a canvas. "But, if it is a drawing for a rock poster I'll refine it even more because that drawing will have a lot of rough edges and be a little messier, having a lot of erase marks. So then I'll scan that again, and retrace a nicer line onto a final piece of paper. Then I make a really tight drawing that will be good for a screen-print."

Nonetheless, Tara wears many hats, being not only a painter and illustrator, but a comic book artist, gig poster artist for rock bands, toy designer and, since 2011, she transformed her Williamsburg studio into the Cotton Candy Machine, a Brooklyn-based retro-style art boutique that serves as a gallery for exhibitions and a showcase for cool merchandise such as books, posters, prints, T-shirts, and toys by Tara and other local talent. She also did a mural in Rome, has done solo gallery presentations and, as if that weren't enough, she has taught in the illustration department at Parsons for 4 years.

Born in San Francisco and raised in Los Angeles, Tara has been drawing

Text continues on page 20

BELOW: *Troubles with Heroes* (2009), oil on linen, 24" x 20", done for the 'Silent Heroes' exhibition at the Iguapop Gallery in Barcelona, Spain.

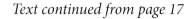

Text continued from page 17

PREVIOUS PAGES SPREAD LEFT:
Untitled (2008), oil, 24" x 30", used also as a gig poster for the Neurosis and Mastodon tour.

PREVIOUS PAGES SPREAD RIGHT:
From the *Seasons* project, we see from left to right, top to bottom, *Spring, Summer, Fall* and *Winter* (2013), oil on linen, each 20" x 24".

BELOW: *Hey We All Die Sometimes* (2008), oil on birch, 24" x 36", from the *Inside Nostalgia* series, this painting is about the aftermath of a relationship...when battle is over and lost.

FACING PAGE: *The Guilt Will Eat You Alive...If You Let It* (2008), oil on birch, 30" x 36", from the *Inside Nostalgia* series, this painting is about keeping secrets and lies inside yourself for too long: if you do, this will happen to you...

since an early age, and like many children wasn't fond of high school. At sixteen she took the High School Proficiency test, and at seventeen went to the Santa Monica Community College. Oddly enough, it wasn't art she took (the Art classes were full) but astronomy and astrophysics: something she has been enthralled with ever since, and that continually shows up in her work. At the same time she also worked in a Japanese anime/toy/art store that turned her on to many artists she had never heard of before. There she discovered the work of Mangaka Katsuya Terada, which led her into Japanese Art and such fine artists as Yoshitomo Nara and Takashi Murakami, anime series like *Ghost in the Shell* and *Neon Genesis Evangelion* and the work of animation master Hayao Miyazaki whose studio *Ghibli* movies she simply adores. She also became fascinated by ukiyo-e woodblock prints and elements of Japanese folklore, including the deep-sea spiritual creatures like the Umibōzu, which pervade some of her paintings. These discoveries rekindled her artistic side once again.

After doing much print making, she reached a crossroads. Asking herself

McPherson

FACING PAGE: *The Fountain*
(2014), oil on birch, 20" x 40",
from the *Supernova* series.
ABOVE: *Supernova* (2014),
oil on birch, 24" x 35", again
featuring some of the classic
trademarks and elements Tara
loves such as deep space,
stars, sparkles, the hollow-
chested girls and water.

what she wanted to do with the rest of her life, she concluded she wanted to be
an artist. "I switched my major back and focused on getting a good portfolio
together so I could apply to a four-year art school. Art Centre College of
Design in Pasadena, California, was like the army. It was really hard work:
deadlines and specific direction. I work really well in that environment,
which is probably why freelancing suits me so fine."

In 2001 she received her BFA with honours from the Art Centre with an
Illustration major and a Fine Art minor. During college, she also interned at
Rough Draft Studios working as a production assistant on Matt Groening's
Futurama series. As to her experience over there she says, "I got paid,
which was awesome. It influenced the way I drew by helping me tighten
up my linework and gave me an insight into the world of animation; how it

ABOVE: *Umibozu Lake* (2014), oil on birch, 24" x 40", from the *Supernova* series, absolutely stunning painting with phosphorescent water and tiny umibôzu spiritual creatures sticking their heads out of the water. Notice that the head is floating without a body over the water. Could it be another sea spirit?

functions and how character designs are made.

"I helped the colourists and got to see how to do turnarounds: creating the front, side, three-quarter and back views of characters. Though I didn't draw anything while I was there, I learned so much."

After college she had free time to do whatever she wanted and, since she was already into rock and heavy metal, began playing bass guitar in a rock band. To announce any live concerts the band obviously needed some flyers, and Tara, being the artist in the group (i.e. she knew how to draw), took care of that aspect. She began with black and white drawings, which she then xeroxed, and this evolved into more detailed colour prints. This also opened up a new opportunity, and she added poster art into her portfolio.

"I listen to music in the studio but, when I'm working on a large show, I tend to get bored towards the end and put on documentaries instead. It's something to think about while I'm painting. I grew up listening to rock and roll, and heavy metal." Since the she has done posters for many and diverse rock bands around the world, and confesses: "That's super-cool to me— my 15-year-old self would've freaked out. I love music and I love art, so it's a perfect marriage of the two, and I get to work in a different way."

By 2004 a new challenge opened up for Tara, and that was doing comic book covers for *Vertigo*, an imprint of *DC* comics specialising in more adult-oriented material. She worked mainly for the *Sandman Presents Thessaly*, and *The Witching* series for which she did countless covers. She would also

ABOVE: *The Water Nebula* (2013), oil on birch, 18" x 18", not from the *Supernova* series, but from the *Wandering Luminations* cycle of the previous year, again with some umibôzu creatures and a siren-like figure emerging from the phosphorescent water and spouting water from the top of her head.

ABOVE: *The Crystal Waterfall*
(2013), oil on wood panel,
30" x 18", from the *Wandering
Luminations* series, full
of phosphorescent light
in deep space.
ABOVE RIGHT: *Cosmic Serpent*
(2013), oil on wood panel,
30" x 24" from the *Wandering
Luminations* series.
FACING PAGE: *Wandering
Luminations* (2013), oil on linen,
stretched over panel, 48" x 36"
from the cycle of the same name
in which Tara's fascination with
science comes again to the fore;
this time through a research she
did on bioluminescence and
the ocean, glow worms,
and ocean creatures.

do an actual comic for the Fables series created by Bill Willingham. The story 'Diaspora' for *Fables: 1001 Nights of Snowfall* was entirely done in acrylics, with each page consisting of a full painting made up with small panels. As to her experience doing that story, Tara says: "The thing is, I like doing covers better than doing comics. I get kind of bored with sequential work. For me it's too much repetition and I need to be more excited about what I'm working on, you know what I mean? The *Fables* thing, that was, like, fourteen pages, so that was perfect. I don't think I could do more than that: I'd need something new!"

Since 2006 she has been publishing through *Dark Horse,* a series of monographic books collecting her artwork. 'Lonely Heart: The Art of Tara McPherson' appeared in 2006, 'Lost Constellations: The Art of Tara McPherson Volume II' in 2009, and the latest, 'Bunny in the Moon: The Art of Tara McPherson Volume III' in 2013.

In 2010 Tara took the next obvious step in her multifarious career, and that was preparing some sculptures of her artwork. This would soon lead to creating toys, which she designed for *Kid Robot* and though many were for known characters, she did manage to leave her indelible imprint on them.

Her art has also appeared on T-shirts, pillow cases, mugs, bags, notebooks,

Text continues on page 32

FACING PAGE: An Interruption of Blood (2015, oil on linen, 18" x 14", created for the Juxtapoz 20th Anniversary show in Los Angeles. LEFT: Acrylic, 15" x 20" (2006). Page 4 from the 'Diaspora' story for the graphic novel *Fables: 1001 Nights of Snowfall* written by Bill Willingham and featuring many other artists as well. Drawing comics wasn't a medium Tara appreciated much, but accepted this project mainly because she loved the series.

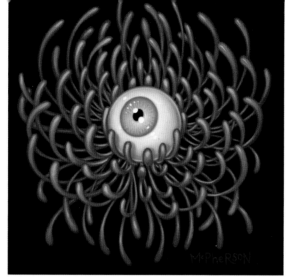

BELOW: *My Love Flows Out Like a Waterfall and Goes Nowhere* (2009), acrylic on birch, 18" x 24", from the *Inside Nostalgia* series.
RIGHT: *The Day's Eye (Chrysanthenum)*, oil on linen, stretched over panel, 9" x 9", from the 2010 series *Bunny in the Moon*, and featuring a strange out-of-this-world flower.

LEFT: *Installation Room*, polyester resin, polyurethane, aluminium, paint, life-size Skull Flowers.
RIGHT: The Wanderers (2013), oil on wood, 24" x 36", from the *Wandering Luminations* series.
BOTTOM: *Lilitu* (2010), oil on linen, 18" x 24", based on the Sumerian myth of demon Lilitu, representing chaos, seduction and ungodliness. Maybe this is what critics and fans refer to as "creepy" in Tara's art.

TOP & BOTTOM LEFT: Two variants for the gig posters for the _Faith No More, Refused_ tour (2013), both four-color screenprints, 18" x 24".
TOP RIGHT: _The Love Note_ (2013), oil on birch, 30" x 18", from the _Wandering Luminations_ series.

Zippo lighters, stickers, etc. As to what lies ahead, Tara likes declares, "I want to continue on this path. I want to create, I want to make fun art and work for awesome bands that I love, but mainly I want to just paint." ●

● _Tara McPherson's website is **www.taramcpherson.com** and you can also visit her online at **www.thecottoncandymachine.com**_

IN THE NEXT ISSUE

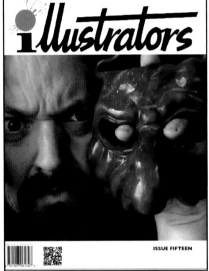

ISSUE FIFTEEN

The art of Dave McKean takes many forms, from painting to sculpture, illustration to film making, always restless, always inventive and always inspiring. Join us as we meet a truly visionary talent.

Ride the high country as we saddle up and join six figure selling artist Andy Thomas for a trip through the old West. Enter the kaleidoscopic world of illustrator/ animator Jonathan Ball and bruise your knuckles with Sam Peffer.

Andy Thomas

Jonathan Ball

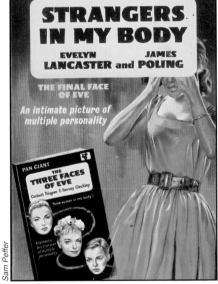

Sam Peffer

Joe Jusko

Follow Diego Cordoba as he tells us about this fantasy artist whose larger than life heroes have graced the covers of all the major comic book companies

PROBABLY ONE OF THE BEST-KNOWN fantasy and comic book cover artists today, Joe Jusko has been actively working as an illustrator for over 30 years. His paintings are rich and vibrant with colour, and peopled by dynamic and vigorous muscular characters that could easily snap a person in half between their thumbs and forefingers.

Born in 1959, Joe grew up on the Lower East Side of New York City, in an area called Alphabet City, consisting of avenues named after the first four letters of the alphabet, and made up mostly of tenement buildings that date back to the 1800s or early 1900s. "Our apartment was in one such tenement, older than old, but it was the best my parents could do," Joe says.

He was inspired at an early age watching his older brother draw. He also discovered comic books, especially those produced by Marvel, which were the first comics he began to seriously collect. Within Marvel he encountered the work of John Buscema, an artist who would have a lasting impression on him. "I had discovered his work in 1968 when I bought second-hand copies of *Avengers* #57 and #58, the first *Vision* story. After that I sought every book

FACING PAGE: T*arzan of the Apes, 100th Anniversary Painting* (2012), acrylics on board.
ABOVE: *Heavy Metal* June 1978, Joe's first cover, painted when he was only 17 and had just graduated from high school.
BELOW: *The Incredible Hulk*, (circa 1997), acrylic on board, painted from a John Buscema pencil drawing for the *Marvel Theme Park* in Florida.

Deathlok © Marvel Entertainment, LLC

he worked on, copying his figures in an attempt to draw with equal facility. Buscema's been my idol since I first realised I could draw and probably the main reason I chose art for a living!"

Knowing pretty early on that his career would be as an illustrator, Joe also discovered that he had a short-attention span, so he'd rather concentrate on a single image than work on a whole comic book.

When it came to choosing a high school, he was coaxed by his 8th grade teachers to attend the High School of Art & Design in Manhattan. Formerly known as the School of Industrial Arts, it was there that he learned the art trade and owed a lot to the highly experienced commercial artists who served as instructors, including *EC* Comics artist Bernie Krigstein.

Joe graduated in 1977 with the *DC* Comics Award of Excellence in Cartooning. "I had begun to paint after graduation. Despite being accepted to every college I applied for, I was not enamoured with the thought of four more years of school and was itching to get my foot in the door…somewhere."

Though he had received an award, he didn't see his future as a comic book

Text continues on page 40

She Hulk © Marvel Entertainment, LLC

RIGHT: Cover to *Dejah Thoris* #1 (2010), acrylic.
FACING PAGE ABOVE: *She-Hulk on Muscle Beach* poster, (1988), acrylic on board.
FACING PAGE BELOW Cover to *Deathlok* #1 (1999), acrylic on board.
FOLLOWING PAGES LEFT: *Primal Pair* (2004), acrylic on board, art for page 35 of the graphic novel, *Tomb Raider: The Greatest Treasure of All*. "My favourite interior page from that comic."
FOLLOWING PAGES RIGHT: *Tarzan in the Baobab* (2009), acrylic on board. Private commission.

Tombb Raider © Top Cow/ Image Comics 2005

FACING PAGE: *Cuddle the Corpse* (2004), acrylic on board, painting for a series of faux 1960s-like paperback covers.
TOP: *Star Trek* (1994), mixed media, featuring the original cast, done as a 3 piece trading card puzzle.
BOTTOM: Cover for *Inferno: Hellbound #1* (2002), acrylic on board.

Text continued from page 36

artist so he used the $25 *Eastern Artist Supplies* gift certificate he had won to buy miscellaneous paints and brushes, and began to train himself as a painter. Luckily for him he also ran into comic book legend Howard Chaykin in a New York comic shop, and Chaykin thought his work was good enough to have him serve as his assistant. Joe's apprenticeship with Chaykin lasted for five months, and through Chaykin he showed his work at *Heavy Metal*, at the time the foremost adult fantasy magazine was printed on slick paper. "Amazingly, editor Julie Simmons actually bought one of my samples and commissioned a second piece, and eventually a third." It seemed the doors into illustration had finally opened up for him, as the first cover he did for *Heavy Metal* had been painted during the summer after graduating from high school when he was only 17!

After his work at *Heavy Metal*, Joe picked up enough courage to contact Rick Marschall, then the editor *Marvel*'s magazine line, for which they also used painted covers. His first cover for *Marvel* was for the *Marvel Preview Presents Starlord #15*, which he considers the worst cover he's ever done! Notwithstanding his thoughts about that first job at *Marvel*, he got to work for them on a run that has lasted to this day.

"I broke in at a time when there weren't a lot of people doing painted work in comics," Joe says. "[At Marvel] I became part of an amazing stable of cover artists that included Earl Norem and Bob Larkin, who was the painter I most admired and wanted to emulate."

However, despite all those covers he was doing, "I wasn't really making a living. I had been working for *Marvel* almost five years and still couldn't afford to move out of my parents' apartment. My mother, as proud as she was that I was doing what I loved, was urging me to get something more stable for a job."

So he became a police officer, his second favourite career, and served in the South Bronx. "The diversity of it was exhilarating, with everything

Text continues on page 45

Spiderman © Marvel Entertainment, LLC

Submariner © Marvel Entertainment, LLC

Conan © Dark Horse Comics Inc.

This page *Marvel Comics* corner boxes
TOP LEFT: *Spiderman* (2015), acrylic on board, after Steve Ditko.
TOP RIGHT: *Sub-Mariner* (2015), acrylic on board, after John Buscema.
BOTTOM: *Conan* (2011), acrylic on board, after John Buscema.

ABOVE: *Dragonfyre*
(1999), acrylic on board,
wraparound cover for *Lady
Pendragon* series. "A limited
palette is a very effective
way to convey mood and
drama in a painting."

Tombb Raider © Top Cow/ Image Comics 2005

44

Text continued from page 40

constantly changing from minute to minute. I've been shot at, slashed at, had both shoulders dislocated at different times, pulled people out of burning buildings and delivered three babies. I loved that job!"

Nonetheless, his true calling was elsewhere, as Joe continues: "After several years I realized art was my main passion and went back to it full time. Luckily, the second time was a charm, and my career took off." "

Since then, he has worked for all the major comic book publishers. Aside from being one of the main cover artists for *The Savage Sword of Conan,* he has also painted every major *Marvel Comics* character. He has also done storyboards for ad agencies and advertising campaigns for such clients as the *World Wrestling Federation.* His fascination with body-building has made him one of the top artists painting larger than life heroes with bulging muscles. So it was a natural for him to do so many *Conan* covers.

"While I've painted hundreds of superhero pieces over the years my main

FACING PAGE: Original art for page 5 of the graphic novel *Tomb Raider: The Greatest Treasure of All* (2005), acrylic on board.
ABOVE: *Jungle apparition* (2000), acrylic on board. Later used as a double page splash for the graphic novel *Tomb Raider: The Greatest Treasure of All.* Not only one of Joe's greatest achievements, but one of the greatest fully-painted graphic novels ever done!

45

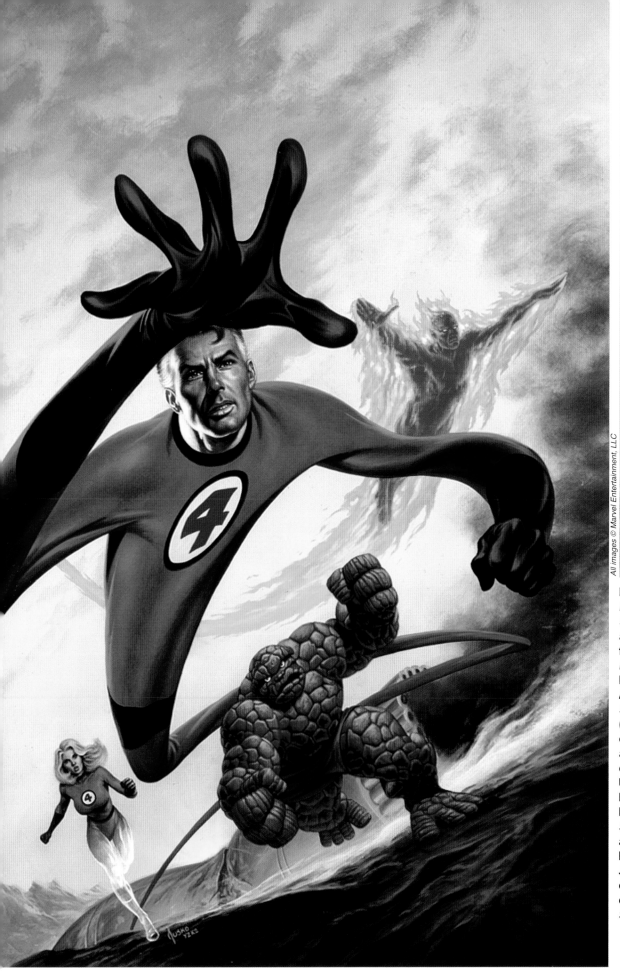

All images © Marvel Entertainment, LLC

LEFT: Cover for
*Marvel Double
Shot* #3 (2003),
acrylic on board,
featuring the
Fantastic Four.
FACING PAGE
ABOVE: *Marvel
Superheroes*
(2007), acrylic
on board. Box
art for the 2008
card set from
Upper Deck.
FACING PAGE
BELOW: *The
Silver Surfer*,
acrylic on
board, after
John Buscema's
classic 1960s
cover for *Silver
Surfer* #1.

interest remains with the more reality-based characters, whether they be horror icons such as *Vampirella* or more adventurous ones like *Lara Croft* or any of those created by the authors Edgar Rice Burroughs or Robert E. Howard. I find them easier to relate to, and they offer the opportunity to paint many of the subjects I found interesting, such as wildlife and natural settings. I'm not a big 'tech' guy so science-fiction is not a favourite subject, unless it's something along the lines of ERB's *John Carter of Mars*, which is much more heroic fantasy than true science-fiction."

In 1992, he painted the Marvel Masterpieces trading card set, which started the whole trading card craze in the '90s, and became the best-selling card set of all time. In 1994 he followed it with the *Art of Edgar Rice Burroughs* trading cards and his work is also featured in Fleer's *Ultra X-Men Wolverine Cards*, as well as the *Conan the Barbarian* and *Vampirella* trading card sets.

In 1995 Joe's first art book, 'Joe Jusko's Art of Edgar Rice Burroughs', was published, making him the artist that has illustrated the greatest number of Burroughs characters. The '90s would also mark his contribution, illustrating *Vampirella*, a female character he's particularly fond of.

"One day back in 1972 I spotted the incredible Enrich cover to *Warren Publishing*'s *Vampirella #21* while perusing my local candy store for the latest comics. I had never before been exposed to the type of art in that magazine,

Text continues on page 52

Satana, Devil's Daughter © Marvel Entertainment, LLC

Rogue © Marvel Entertainment, LLC

Daredevil © Marvel Entertainment, LLC

Images from the 2016 *Marvel Masterpieces* card set.
FACING PAGE: *Satana, Devil's Daughter* (2014), acrylic.
TOP LEFT: *Rogue* (2014), acrylic.
TOP RIGHT: *Daredevil* (2015), acrylic.
BOTTOM RIGHT: *Fin Fang Foom* (2014), acrylic.
BOTTOM LEFT: *Spiderman* (2015), acrylic. "The original
1992 *Marvel Masterpieces* card set is the most popular
thing I've ever done and this follow up is my most
eagerly anticipated job In years. It totally blows the first
set out of the water as far as finish and quality!"

Spiderman © Marvel Entertainment, LLC

Fin Fang Foom © Marvel Entertainment, LLC

49

Conan © Dark Horse Comics Inc.

Wonder Woman © DC Comics

FACING PAGE: *Restful Interlude* (2007), acrylic on board. Cover for the 'Art of Joe Jusko' book from *Desperado Publishing*.
ABOVE LEFT: *Next?* (1999), acrylic on board. Concept design and box for a statue that was never produced.
ABOVE RIGHT: *Wonder Woman* (1999), acrylic on board. "Done for my own amusement several years back."
LEFT: Wraparound cover for *Warlord of Mars #4* (2010), acrylic on board. "Loved painting the Martian lions called *Banths*."

51

ABOVE: *Dejah Thoris #8* (2011), acrylic on *Crescent* #100 cold-pressed illustration board. Cover printed on its side for *Warlord* #6.
FACING PAGE: Crossover cover for *Warlord of Mars* #28 (2012), acrylic on board. "Easily one of my favorite covers from the run so far!"
BELOW: Cover to 'Fall of Barsoom' #2 (2011). acrvlic on board.

Text continued from page 47

art that was so much more illustrative than that in the average comic book. I was enamoured by the beauty of José Gonzalez's art on the *Vampirella* strip (as well as the many other brilliant artists within the covers), and by the aesthetic appeal and Gothic romance of the character herself. I bought all of the back issues I had missed and every subsequent issue from then on. I had always hoped to add my work to the brilliant pantheon of *Warren* artists but *Warren Publishing* went out of business soon after I entered the field, and I thought any chance of that was lost.

"Luckily, *Harris Comics* bought the rights to the character and I began a 20 year association with them, painting a great many covers and one fully-painted graphic novel. Some things were just meant to be, it seems."

Among some of his most recent work is the absolutely astonishing fully-painted graphic novel based on *Lara Croft*, the heroine from the *Tomb Raider* video games. It wasn't the first time he tackled 'drawing' a comic book, but 'Tomb Raider: The Greatest Treasure of All' is one of the best such jobs, done in a particularly different and difficult way. Painted with acrylics on illustration board, the job has been "without doubt the most work I've ever put into anything and the best work I've ever done!" Nonetheless the years he put into that project paid off in the end, for it won him a Certificate

Vampirella © Dynamite Entertainment

ABOVE: Cover to *Warlord of Mars* #14 (2011), acrylic on board.
TOP RIGHT: *Sad Wings of Destiny* (1995), acrylic on board. "By far one of my most popular Vampi pieces!"
FACING PAGE: *Queens of Darkness and Light* (2015), acrylic on board.
BOTTOM: Crossover cover for *Hack/Slash meets ReAnimator* (2008), acrylic on board.

of Merit from the prestigious *Society of Illustrators* (which accepted him as a member in 2007).

For *Dynamite Entertainment* he has been doing covers for their Burroughs' Mars series, featuring *John Carter* and *Dejah Thoris*. The 'Art of Joe Jusko' book, collecting some of the various paintings he has done throughout his career, was published to rave reviews by *Desperado Publishing* in 2009, and saw a second printing from *IDW* in 2012.

His art is also featured in the *Dynamite* hardcover books 'Art of Dejah Thoris and the Worlds of Mars' and 'Art of Vampirella: The Dynamite Years'.

Joe's incredible talent has won him a multitude of awards, starting with the *Comic Buyer's Guide Fan Award* for 'Favourite Painter' in 1992 and 1993; the *Wizard Fan Award* for 'Favourite Painter' in 1993 and 1994; multiple trading card awards, and a *Golden Lion Award* from the *Burroughs Bibliophiles*.

"I'm a totally self-taught painter who grew up reading comics and who broke into that field at the same time I was first learning to paint. As such, my palettes and colour schemes emulated the comics I was reading up to that time and many times were incredibly garish and amateurish. It took me years, and years, to learn to control my palette, until today where I can alter it to properly suit whatever property on which I'm working. For instance, my *Tarzan* paintings have a much more natural palette than the *John Carter* pieces, since Mars is described by Burroughs as having a 9 colour spectrum as opposed to our 7 colour. I still paint the superhero pieces with heightened palette as I can't see them as real people in the muted palettes that have

ABOVE: *The Oz/Wonderland Chronicles* (2006), acrylics on board, from the series of the same name, a modern take on the tales of Alice and Dorothy. **RIGHT:** *Peace on Earth* (2001), acrylic on board. "Painted shortly after 9/11 as my personal Christmas card in 2001 symbolizing mankind and nature coexisting as one."

become the accepted norm today. They will always be comic book characters to me and painting them in a very hyper-realistic manner loses the magic that made them seem special and magical to me as a kid."

His influences over the years have come from myriad places. "Early on I was influenced by all the usual ones you'd suspect: Frank Frazetta, Boris Vallejo, Enric, Sanjulian, Bob Larkin, James Bama. All the genre guys who worked within my field. As time goes on, and my interests widened, so did my influences. I began to look at '50s & '60s paperback and magazine artists like Robert McGinnis, Al Parker, Robert Maguire, Ron Lesser, and wildlife painters such as John Seerey-Lester, Simon Combes and Guy Coheleach. The worst thing an artist can do is close his eyes to anything outside of his own discipline." ●

● *You can see more of Joe's work on his official website:* ***www.joejusko.com*** *or on his DeviantArt page:* ***joejusko.deviantart.com*** *and follow him on Twitter at:* ***twitter.com/joejusko***

Fortunino Matania (1881-1963) signed prints

In a British Advanced Observation Post (signed print 1918)

Somewhere in France: A Concert Behind Enemy Lines (signed print 1918)

Coming in 2016 the definitive Matania art book
Drawing From History: The Art of Fortunino Matania

IllustrationArtGallery.com
The world's largest gallery of original illustration and comic strip art
Tel: 020 8768 0022 (from outside UK+44 20 8768 0022) E: art@illustrationartgallery.com

Maurice Leloir

David Ashford draws aside the curtains on the majesterial world of Maurice Leloir, whose sumptuous art brought to life stories of France's rich and colourful imperial history.

IN 1893, WHEN THE SON OF ALEXANDRE DUMAS decided that a lavish illustrated edition of his father's immortal story, *The Three Musketeers*, was long overdue, he felt that there was only one illustrator who could do the novel justice and that man was Maurice Leloir. Not only was Leloir amply fitted for the task through his professional accomplishments as an illustrator on such works as 'Manon Lascaut', 'The Sentimental Journey' and 'The Confessions of Jean-Jacques Rousseau', but also because he was a widely recognised expert on the

FACING PAGE: A breathtaking scene from 'Richelieu', published in 1901.
ABOVE TOP: Louis XIV's summoning of the State General is captured in this illustration from 'Le Roy Soleil' published in 1904.
ABOVE: 'The Three Musketeer's' from 1893.

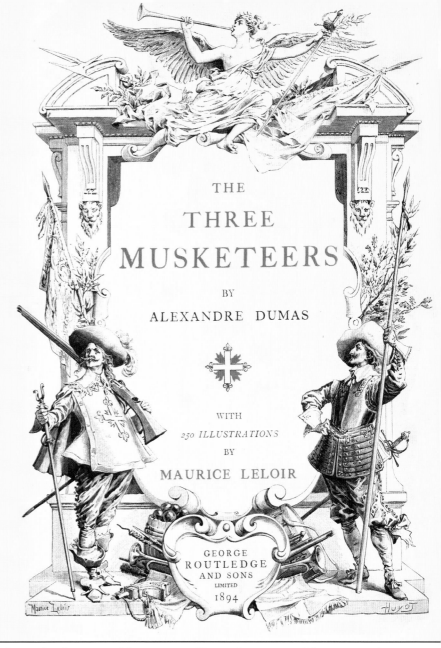

ABOVE: Such was the power of Leloir's visualisations that Douglas Fairbanks commissioned him to design the sets for *The Iron Mask*.
RIGHT: The title page to 'The Three Musketeers.
FACING PAGE: Clouds of smoke provide a neat metaphor for the Cardinal's scheming. 'Richelieu' 1901.

history of costume. It is also noteworthy that Leloir's father, himself an historical painter, had been a personal friend of Alexandre Dumas.

Maurice Leloir produced 250 pen and ink drawings of the finest quality for this two volume edition of 'The Three Musketeers', published the following year, 1894. On completing the work, he wrote to Alexandre Dumas Fils: "For two years I have been living with D'Artagnan, Athos, Porthos, Aramis, and the many personages of that great epopee. I trust that I may soon meet them again in 'Twenty Years After'!" (Leloir was referring to the sequel to 'The Three Musketeers', which, unfortunately, was never to be included in these illustrated editions.) It was Leloir's depictions, in these two volumes of Dumas' epic of adventure, that were to establish forever in the public's mind the look of these Musketeers and, indeed, all the other characters in Dumas' novel.

When Douglas Fairbanks, at the time the most powerful star in Hollywood, conceived his screenplay for 'The Iron Mask', based on Dumas' 'The Three Musketeers', 'The Man in the Iron Mask and The Memoirs of D'Artagnan', he was insistent that no expense should be spared to create the proper period atmosphere for this movie. He decided to travel to Paris personally to consult the celebrated Dumas illustrator, Maurice Leloir. The result was that Leloir was contracted to come to Hollywood for five months to design the entire film.

The Iron Mask, the last of Fairbanks' silent movies, was released in February, 1929. In the opening credits the following bold statement is made, which clearly shows just how highly Leloir was rated as an artist of truly international status: "This entire production was under the supervision of Maurice Leloir, Member of the Society of French Artists, illustrator of 'The Three Musketeers'; the acknowledged authority on the period depicted." Leloir wrote a fascinating book about

« Instructions et maximes qu'il s'est données pour se conduire à la cour »,
parfait bréviaire de l'ambitieux et du courtisan.

Les efforts de l'évêque de Luçon ne restent pas stériles. Sa
réputation grandit. On parle de lui, même chez
le roi.

Pour paraître et se produire, il n'attend plus
qu'une occasion, la guette non sans impatience.

ABOVE: Leloir's depiction of Alexandre Dumas, one of 250 illustrations that he produced for the two volume edition of 'The Three Musketeers".
ABOVE RIGHT: Leloir's mastery of recreating moments from history is well to the fore in this spread from 'Le Roy Soleil'.
RIGHT PAGE: A visceral fight to the death from 'The Three Musketeers' is neatly contrasted with Leloir's attention to period furnishing. His sublime figurework was complimented by his ability to create entirely convincing environments.

his Hollywood experiences, titled 'My Five Months in Hollywood', published the year of the film's release.

I first came across the art of Maurice Leloir in a copy of 'The Three Musketeers' in the library of Leonard Matthews, erstwhile editor-in-chief of Juvenile Publications at Fleetway House. He himself had scripted picture strip versions of Dumas' tale for three publications under his control, as well as overseeing all the Musketeer tales in the *Thriller Comics Library*. Looking at these illustrations, it immediately became apparent to me that Leonard had used Leloir's pictures to inspire his artists. It was not long before I had acquired the two volume 1894 English Edition de Luxe limited edition of "750 Numbered Copies, and 25 Unnumbered Copies, for the United Kingdom and the British Colonies". Not long after, the same friend who had purchased these volumes for me came across another Leloir-illustrated book, set in the same period but this time lavishly illustrated in

full colour: 'Richelieu'. Published in 1901, is a large and particularly sumptuous volume, containing forty chromotypogravure watercolours, including thirty four full page and two double page plates. Once again, Leloir portrays the Romantic world of Dumas' Musketeers, and brings to life all the vitality and grandeur of 17th century France.

Maurice Leloir was born in Paris on November 1st 1853, and died in the same city on October 7th 1940. He was fortunate to have been born into a family of highly successful artists: Maurice's father was the historical painter, Jean-Baptiste Auguste Leloir, and his mother, Héloïse Colin, was a watercolourist and miniaturist. Héloïse was also the daughter of the renowned Romantic painter of historical and genre subjects, Alexandre Marie Colin, who was a close friend and associate of Eugène Delacroix. Maurice's older brother, Louis, was also a successful artist who, in 1861, was the winner of

63

FACING PAGE: Deadly sport—an illustration from 'Richelieu' provides yet another glimpse into the mores of 17th century France.
BELOW: Swashbuckling and derring do—two more illustrations from 'The Three Musketeers'. The commission took Leloir two years to complete.

the highly prestigious Prix de Rome. Maurice's career would be closely associated with that of his brother up until Louis' early death in 1884.

Maurice was only in his early twenties when, in 1875, he first exhibited his work at the renowned Salon de Paris, where he became a member. Then, in 1878, together with his brother Louis and many other renowned painters, Maurice collaborated in the foundation of the Society of French Watercolourists. From this time on he decided to turn his back on the Salon de Paris and dedicate himself to the art of painting in watercolour and, particularly the illustration of historical novels. It would not be long before he became one of the most sought-after illustrators for the new growing market for lavishly illustrated books.

The books he illustrated from about 1883 onwards accurately represent the costumes and attitudes of the past, especially the elegant and mannered fashions of the 17th and 18th centuries in France. Leloir by this time had acquired one of the finest collections of historic costumes imaginable for use in his illustrations but, impeccable draughtsman that he was, his models never

look as though they are in fancy dress but real men and women of the period. A later French critic observed: "It is the very soul of the 18th century that vibrates in his delicate watercolours". One could add that this applied even more so to his watercolour and black and white illustrations of the 17th century.

The majority of the books that Leloir illustrated were produced to the highest level of book design and the reproduction of his work, whether in black and white, line drawing or watercolour painting, benefitted enormously from first class printing and, in particular, from the supremely talented French engravers that were among the finest in the world.

As far as his forays into the world of book illustration were concerned, the year 1885 was a very rewarding one for Maurice Leloir. That year he contributed twelve full page compositions and 220 drawings in the text (all in black and white) for Laurence Sterne's classic 18th century novel 'A Sentimental Journey'. The illustrations were well received, but even more successful was his work for an 1885 edition of the novel 'Manon Lescaut' by the Abbé Prévost. The illustrations were again all in black

LEFT: Two illustrations from 'Manon Lescaut'. Provost's tragic tale was well known amongst the Parisian cultural elite, having been adapted as a hugely successful opera by Massenet. Leloir, who was well known for his poster designs for Massenet, was the logical choice to illustrate the book.

ABOVE: Leloir turned the climactic scene of the Chevalier des Grieux with his dead lover Manon, in the Louisiana wilderness, into a searing and powerful oil painting which was rapturously received when it was presented at the 1892 Paris Salon.

Dahesh Museum of Art, New York. 2001.12

and white, consisting of twelve full page engravings and no less than 225 vignettes and ornaments, full of the most exquisite detail and atmosphere.

The year before, Jules Massenet's opera based on the novel had premiered to great success in Paris and, Leloir, being known for his poster designs for Massenet's operas, was the obvious choice to illustrate the new edition of Provost's tragic tale. Later Leloir based one of his most famous oil paintings on one of the images he drew for the book: the penultimate scene depicting the Chevalier des Grieux with his dead lover, Manon, in the wilderness of Louisiana. Leloir presented his oil version of 'Manon Lescaut' at the 1892 Paris Salon to great acclaim, and, in the following year (the same year Puccini's opera *Manon Lescaut* premiered in Turin), it was shown at the Chicago World's Colombian Exposition.

Splendid as the 'Manon Lescaut' illustrations were, the book that brought out the very best in Leloir was Dumas' 'The Three Musketeers'. It is widely recognised that the 250 black and white drawings he did for the deluxe 1893 version are unsurpassed for their acute sense of period and for the historically accurate detail of costumes, arms and equipment, and architecture.

There is no doubt that it was Maurice Leloir's illustrations that brought to life all the marvellous characters of Dumas' romance and, stamped their likenesses onto our consciousness for all time.

Here are Dumas' Musketeers in all their swagger and warm-hearted camaraderie, and here is Cardinal Richelieu in all his power and duplicity together with the beautiful but deadly Milady de Winter. Every one of the many characters is portrayed with absolute understanding and genuine affection. These illustrations are bold, expressive and full of the true romance of the period, depicting the roistering panache of the Musketeers contrasted with the dark, scheming intrigues of the Cardinal and Milady. And, of course, there is much action here as well, which Leloir handles with dexterous ability. Looking at these images one can't help feeling that the artist revelled in this particular commission. As Leloir told Dumas' son, he looked forward to meeting the Musketeers again in the sequel, 'Twenty Years After'. He must have been extremely disappointed when that wish remained unfulfilled.

As if in consolation, in 1903 Leloir was given the opportunity of illustrating, again in black and white,

ABOVE LEFT: Another scene from 'Manon Lescaut', as the star-crossed lovers find that dreams of elopement are as naught. The story was so popular that it spawned three operas, with versions by Auber and Puccini as well as Massanet's.

ABOVE & FACING PAGE: Leloir's work was familiar to a wide audience appearing in books, magazines, posters and advertising art, and his signature could be seen on the labels for Bénédictine liqueur, Calvet wine, Clicquot champagne and Planteur chocolate. The income from his endeavours enabled him to live amongst the upper echelons of Parisian society

ENTRÉE DE LOVIS XIV ROY DE FRANCE ET DE MARIE THÉRÈSE D'AVSTRICHE REYNE DE FRANCE, A PARIS EN MDCLX

another Dumas novel, 'La Dame de Monsoreau'. Set in 16th century France, the story enabled Leloir to convey all the hauteur and elegance of the court of Henri III. Next to the excitement and dynamism of his images for 'The Three Musketeers', however, while admitting to a certain disappointment in the illustrations for this novel, there is still, nevertheless, much to be admired. There is one double page spread that is particularly noteworthy: The image portrays the spectacle of Henri III being escorted through the streets of Paris, and the one detail that immediately captures our attention is the King's extraordinary-looking coach. Only Leloir, the most meticulously exact of all historical illustrators, could have convinced us of its authenticity. But this is

ABOVE: Further evidence of Leloir's phenomenal grasp of period and place with his depiction of the entry of Louis XIV and his wife Marie Therese into the city of Paris. From 'Le Roy Soleil', 1904. RIGHT: Louis XIII visits a visibly ailing Richelieu, from the final full page illustration in 'Richelieu', published in 1901.

a man who not only knew all there was to know about historical costume, but also everything pertaining to the period in question—and that included the vehicles used.

Maurice Leloir always thought of himself as primarily a watercolourist, and his proficiency in this medium can be seen to advantage in his illustrated volumes, 'Richelieu' and 'The Sun King', both pertaining to his beloved 17th century France. The latter contains some colourful scenes set inside the Palace of Versailles and in the Royal Gardens, as well as a two page panorama depicting the entry of the 'Sun King', Louis XIV, and Marie Therese, his Austrian wife, into the city of Paris, cheering crowds thronging the route. However, judged by modern tastes, these watercolour illustrations have a tendency towards sentimentality. They are lacking the vigour we expect from Leloir. The same certainly can't be said for the watercolour images he contributed to 'Richelieu'. Here is Leloir at his best. The illustrations are strong and vibrant with a powerful sense of space, composition and colour. The illustrations in this book demonstrate all his abilities for evoking atmosphere, mood and historical veracity.

Apart from his work in book illustration, and his contributions to prestigious magazines such as *'Figaro Illustre,* Leloir's reputation as the specialist in authentic

BELOW: Another scene from Douglas Fairbanks' production of 'The Man in the Iron Mask'. A film which bears the stamp of Leloir's artistry and to which he contributed many set and costume designs.
RIGHT: 'Conversation galante au Hameau' Although much of Leloir's work was in line and watercolour, his command of oil paint and his feeling for light were equally assured.

historical illustration brought him many financially rewarding commissions from some unusual sources. From the 1880s through to the 1920s, his work could be found in publicity material for hotels, high class grocers and even novelty manufacturers. Leloir's signature could be seen on the labels for Bénédictine liqueur, Calvet wine, Clicquot champagne and Planteur chocolate. In 1903, he was commissioned to design 18th century scenes of the Trianon and Versailles for the salon of the Villa Tijuca at Saint-Jean Cap Ferrat and, in 1923, he designed scenes from the period of Louis XIV for the ceiling and friezes of the Marquise de Sevigne's celebrated Parisian tea rooms on the Boulevard de la Madeleine.

As a collector of historical costumes, Leloir contributed to a number of exhibitions and regional museums, but his grand idea was his creation of a costume museum in Paris. In 1907 he founded the Society of Costume History and, as president, supervised the restoration of costumes, weapons and even ancient vehicles that were bought or given to them. Later, in 1920, Leloir gifted to the Carnavalet Museum in Paris 2,000 costumes and accessories. One of his greatest achievements was his

'Dictionary of Costume and Accessories, Weapons and Fabrics, from its Origins to Today'. Written and illustrated by Leloir, it was published after his death in 1951. This Dictionary remains a major reference for all those who study historical costume.

It's not overstating the case to say that Maurice Leloir was an artist truly obsessed with the past. His life was dedicated to the idea of resurrecting the past in every aspect of historical art. In everything he did, from advertising, promotion material and magazine work, to his gallery painting, designs for Parisian interiors and, especially, his work for books, he revealed a true appreciation of the importance of authenticity in historical illustration. It was his great skill as a draughtsman and watercolourist that enabled Leloir to bring his perception and vision of the past so vividly to life.●

● *I would like to thank my good friend, Mike Crowley, for his invaluable help in translating for me a number of French articles on Leloir.*

DAHESH MUSEUM OF ART

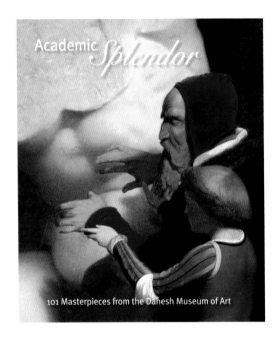

Rediscover the Splendors of
Academic Art from the
Dahesh Museum of Art

View the Collection and shop the
Museum's publications online at
www.daheshmuseum.org

145 Avenue of the Americas, New York, NY 10013

The Studio: Adam Stower

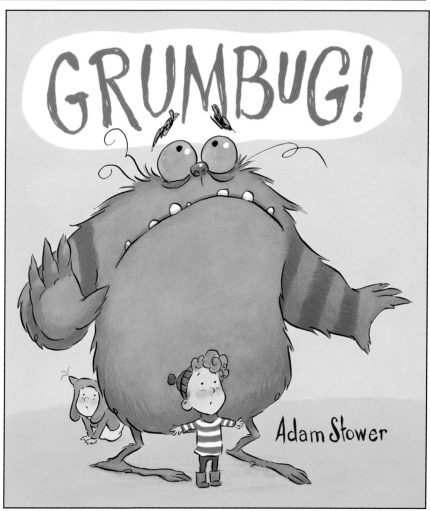

ABOVE: Meeting and greeting plays an important part in the lives of many children's book creatives—Adam's career has literally taken him around the world as he shares his storytelling and art with his many followers.
ABOVE RIGHT AND FACING PAGE: Adam's delightful creations 'Troll and the Oliver' make their reappearance in 'Grumbug', *Templar Publishing* 2015.

The work of Brighton-based artist Adam Stower is underpinned by exquisite draftsmanship and superb observational skills. His art is narrative driven and full of charm and incident. Peter Richardson had the pleasure of interviewing Adam and discovering a lot more about his art and what makes him tick.

PR: Did you always draw?
AS: Yes. I have enjoyed drawing for as long as I can remember. The first illustration of mine to appear in print was a cartoon of a high jumper. It was published in my school magazine. I was only nine, but I remember very clearly the excitement I felt seeing the published drawing. Perhaps that was the moment I was bitten by the illustration bug.

PR: Were any other members of your family artistic?
AS: Both of my grandfathers were very artistic: My grandad Sam was an architect and a wonderful draughtsman. He was the architect responsible for London Bridge. My grandad Bill was an accomplished amateur painter and photographer. My mother has always been very creative too, and dad

has recently taken up woodturning.

PR: Where did you train?

AS: I never did Art A Level but managed to get on to the foundation course in Art and Design at the Cambridge College of Arts and Technology (now Anglia Ruskin University) on the strength of my O level art work. I was very lucky, and I have been thankful of that moment ever since. From there I went to the Norwich School of Arts to undertake a degree in Illustration, and then onto Brighton University for a Masters Degree in Narrative Illustration. I never left Brighton: I still live and work here by the sea.

PR: What were your early influences?

AS: There are some picture books that I remember vividly from my childhood: 'In the Night Kitchen' by Maurice Sendak: 'The Sorceror's Apprentice' by Tomi Ungerer and 'Captain Slaughterboard Drops Anchor', by Mervyn Peake to name but a few. I can see elements in my work that echo those books, even now. It always amazes me how powerful our first experiences of books can be, and I try to keep that in mind when I make my own picture books.

At college, I discovered all the classic book illustrators who were very influential for me, including Arthur Rackham, Edmund Dulac, Heath Robinson etc. Then there was Ronald Searle, Heinrich Kley, Windsor McCay, early Disney…The list goes on.

PR: Did drawing come easily to you?

AS: Yes, I have always felt very comfortable drawing. Like any creative pursuit, the hard part is putting in the hours of practice, but if you love the activity of drawing then that hard work becomes a pleasure. I draw as often as I can, whether from life or my imagination. I like to experiment too: There is always more to learn.

PR: Did you find it difficult to break into illustration?

AS: No. Because my work has always been based on a foundation of traditional drawing, I was able to be quite versatile stylistically. This served me well in those early years. I was happy to take on any job, from wine labels to leaflets about the perils of hypertension, and I managed to earn a living from illustration from the outset. However, the downside to versatility is that it takes longer to establish a style that is unique and recognizable as one's own.

PR: What sort of work did you do to begin with?

AS: I did a lot of work for educational publishing in those early days. It wasn't very glamorous but it was a wonderful apprenticeship of sorts. It often forced me out of my comfort zone, and it taught me to work to a brief and to a deadline. It provided me with valuable experience that has helped me throughout my career.

PR: Did you always have a strong sense of the work you wanted to do?

AS: During my time working for educational publishing, the jobs I enjoyed most were for fiction. It was clear to me that narrative illustration was the area I found most compelling and rewarding. I knew that ultimately I wanted to write and illustrate my own picture books. I am fascinated by picture books as an art form, and the challenge of telling stories through the balance of words and pictures. I am happy to say that almost all of what I do now is for picture books and children's fiction.

PR: Did you find it easy moving to creating art on the computer?

AS: Most of my work is still created by hand but there are some jobs I do partly or completely digitally. In those instances the shift has been gradual, from using the Mac to tweak work, then scanning in hand drawn line art and colouring it digitally, to finally creating the entire illustration with a *Wacom* tablet and *Photoshop*. Ultimately

ABOVE AND FACING PAGE: Adam Stower's illustrations for 'Mrs. Noodlekugel' ooze charm and personality. Published in 2012 by *Candlewick Press*, the art provides an exemplar of how great illustration compels the viewer to engage with the text.

though, I prefer not to have to stare at a screen all day, and I am too in love with creating art by hand to ever relinquish it entirely.

PR: What are the advantages and disadvantages that you have encountered in working digitally?

AS: I do a weekly cover illustration for *Money Week* magazine. This is an example of a job that I now do entirely on the computer. Working digitally offers a speed and flexibility that is an enormous advantage for these illustrations. I am commissioned on a Tuesday afternoon for a Wednesday morning delivery.

I enjoy experimenting on the computer and using what I learn in my hand drawn work. It is very much a two-way street.

I think one of the disadvantages of the digital option is that it makes it very easy to produce an illustration that looks quite nice. What I mean is that it can be a very tempting short cut for new illustrators. There is a danger that the work produced lacks soul. There are many amazing digital illustrators out there producing wonderful work, but I would encourage new artists to develop good drawing skills first, which will act as a strong foundation for all future work in whichever medium they choose, digital or otherwise.

PR: Would you say it is easier to make illustration a career since you started?

LEFT AND FACING PAGE: Although Adam generates the majority of his work employing traditional methods, his cover work for *Money Week* is created entirely on the computer to accommodate a brief that arrives on a Tuesday afternoon for a Wednesday morning delivery.

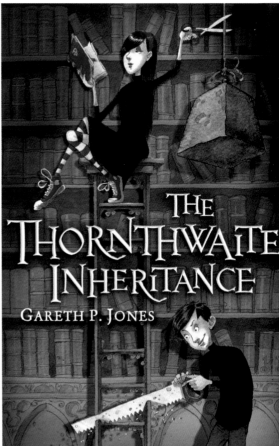

ABOVE: A superbly dark and ironic cover for Gareth P. Jones 'The Thornthwaite Inheritance', published by *Bloomsbury Publishing* in 2009.

AS: Making a career of illustration has never been easy. I think that these days modern technology offers illustrators exciting new ways to create and present their work. There is a healthy appetite for all things creative, and hopefully many opportunities for illustrators to flourish. However, I think the toughest challenge for new illustrators these days is to stand out from the crowd. There are so many new illustrators emerging each year: It has become harder to be noticed.

PR: What advice would you give to people trying to make a career of illustration?

AS: I said it earlier, but I will say it again: Learn to draw. It is fundamental to everything else. Be the best at what you do. Love what you do. Always go the extra mile when sending in samples of work to publishers. Add personal touches. Make your submission special. Do your research. Do not submit work to clients who will have no use for it, it will waste your time and theirs. Seek inspiration from everything around you, but particularly from things unique to you, and from what you find fascinating. It will help you develop your own voice, your own way of doing things. This will help you produce the best work you can and stand out from the crowd. Be tenacious. Develop your own side projects during any gaps in work, whether they are picture book ideas, cards, prints, pottery, anything. It will all feed back in to your main work. And while I am at it, don't forget to exercise. It jogs ideas loose

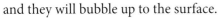
and they will bubble up to the surface.

PR: Do you think it is necessary for people wanting to work as professional illustrators to undertake a degree in illustration?

AS: It isn't necessary as such, but I do think it is advisable. Spending time in a supportive and inspiring environment with like-minded people gives you the opportunity to discover a way of working that is unique to you. Having the equipment, facilities and tutors on hand is invaluable too. I would recommend it to anyone hoping to pursue a career as an illustrator. I had an amazing time at college. Much of what I learnt there was from my fellow students as well as from the staff.

PR: Have you any projects that you are particularly pleased with?

AS: In 2011 I wrote and illustrated 'Silly Doggy!', a picture book published by Templar. In this book I tried to encapsulate what I particularly enjoy about picture books, namely using the interplay of words and pictures to tell a story in the most effective way.

'Silly Doggy' is the story of a little girl called Lily who is delighted to find a 'Silly Doggy!' in her garden. They spend the day together

FACING PAGE: A delightfully wacky image from Adam's self-penned 'Troll and the Oliver', published in 2013 by *Templar Publishing.*
ABOVE: A selection of darkly Gothic images from the 'Keyholders' series published in 2009 by *Starscape Books.*

THIS PAGE & FACING PAGE: Artwork and a cover for 'Silly Doggy', Adam's delightful and engaging story about a little girl and her newly adopted pet. Published by *Templar Publishing* in 2011, it has become a firm favourite with children and parents and has been featured on *BBC TV's CBeebies*.

And a bit grumpy, too.

but are ultimately parted when the owners respond to a poster Lily has made, and come to fetch 'Silly Doggy!' home again. Lily's sadness is soon abated when, the next morning, she finds a 'Silly Kitty!' in her garden.

It is a simple story, but when we add the illustrations, we discover that 'Silly Doggy' is in fact a bear. Suddenly the story is full of tension, humour and surprise.

At no point in the text do I mention that 'Silly Doggy' is a bear. The result is a story with a pantomime feel to it. The reader knows something the main character does not. It is great fun to read aloud to children at school visits and festivals. They can clearly see what 'Silly Doggy' is but despite their frustrated shouts of "IT'S A BEAR!", I refuse to admit it. It drives them bonkers. The pay off at the end is 'Silly Kitty' turns out to be a tiger. The book was a challenge to get right but I am very happy with the result.

PR: Have you any projects that turned into a nightmare?

AS: I have been doing this for over 20 years now and although there have been a few hairy moments there aren't any that I would describe as a nightmare. The bumps that illustrators usually face are things like tight deadlines, tricky and picky clients who don't have a clear idea of what they want; clients who expect work on spec for no fee, or poorly briefed work that turns out to be very different in nature to what you were originally led to believe. These are all easy to handle in of themselves, but if a few of them happen collectively

Photo by Mary Morgan-Stower

BELOW: One of Adam's more recent commissions—the cover to *Macmillan*'s republished 'Just William'. Richmal Crompton's charming delinquent has seldom looked better. Adam's art, with its idiosyncratic line and two colour styling, is the perfect mix of retro styling and contemporary charm.

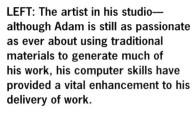

LEFT: The artist in his studio—although Adam is still as passionate as ever about using traditional materials to generate much of his work, his computer skills have provided a vital enhancement to his delivery of work.

ABOVE: 'Crimebiters! My Dog Is Better Than Your Dog''. Written by Tommy Greenwald and published by *Scholastic Press* in 2015.
ABOVE RIGHT: Adam's cover art for his 'Troll and the Oliver'.

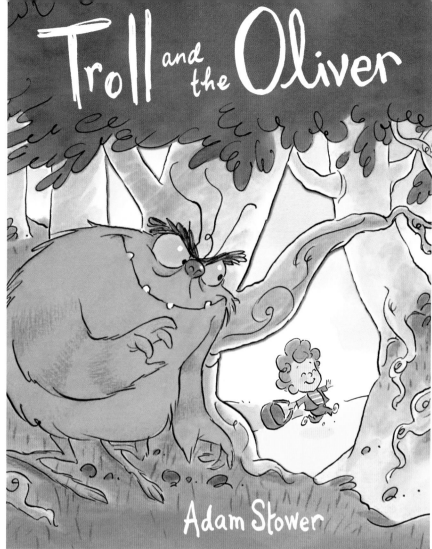

on one job, you start to enter that nightmare territory. Good luck!

PR: What would you like to work on for the future?

AS: I have a few more picture book ideas bubbling away, so I look forward to working on those. I am currently writing my first illustrated chapter book for older children, and with a little luck I might be writing more of those too. My book 'Troll and the Oliver' (Templar, 2013), has been picked up by an animation company for possible development into a film, which is very exciting. I love animation and I would love to work on the film in some capacity if it proceeds. There's a lot to look forward to.

PR: If you were starting out all over again, would you still make illustration your career?

AS: Yes, absolutely. I can't think of anything else I would want to do. It has surprises in store too. Besides my time in the studio, I have had the pleasure of being invited to literary festivals as far afield as Cape Town: I have run sketch clubs and kids clubs in the Caribbean and visited schools from Durham to Geneva, and all in the last year. I feel very lucky to be doing what I do, and to be a part the community of illustrators here and abroad.●

● *For more of Adam's enchanting art check out his website at:*
www.worldofadam.com.
He is also represented by Arena Illustrators and his page is at:
arenaillustration.com/portfolios/adam-stower

Maurice Leloir (1853-1940) Original Art

Richelieu book illustration 1910
Mixed media signed upper left

IllustrationArtGallery.com

The world's largest gallery of illustration paintings and comic strips
Tel: 020 8768 0022 (from outside UK+44 20 8768 0022) E: art@illustrationartgallery.com

Out There: Mike Zagorski

ABOVE: 'Sexy Slayer': dominant women, dinosaurs and decorous female feet are recurring themes in much of Mike's work.
RIGHT & FACING PAGE: The iconography of Zagorski's art draws deeply on comics and movies, but the intensity of his vision is devoid of any artifice. His work is compelling and compulsive—a true one-off.

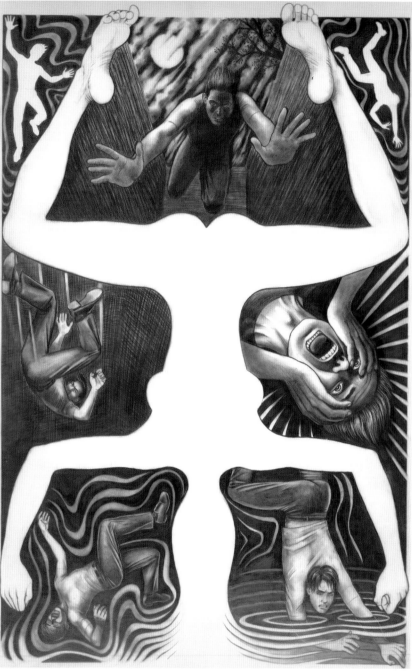

Mike Zagorski is an artist whose illustrations are so guilelessly weird that they compel the viewer to take a second and even a third look. His passion for his subject matter is such that his drawings are imbued with an intensity that immediately transmits itself to his audience. Join with us as we delve a little deeper into the work of a truly remarkable artist.

MIKE ZAGORSKI IS A COMPLETE ONE-OFF, the kind of impassioned and compulsive artist that we at *Illustrators* just love to check out. He was introduced to us by Ron Murphy aka 'Arty Freeman', who has known Mike for over thirty years. It's also worth mentioning that 'Arty Freeman' is another artistic one-off, who in turn was introduced to us by the legendary "World's Best Artist" Mitch O'Connell. As the saying goes, "It takes one to know one!".

As Ron relates, "the first time that I ever went over to

ABOVE: 'Witch'; the richness of Mike's visions lend a surreal intensity to his subjects.
RIGHT & FACING PAGE: Two images from an unpublished comic that Mitch O' Connell, Ron Murphy and Mike collaborated on. Homages to Tor Johnson and Betty Page abound.

his house…the very first things that I noticed were the small green plastic army men figures on Mike's shelf, that were all sporting (real) grasshopper heads, as well as real insect wings mounted onto their backs…Mike has a total obsession with collecting insects: a beautiful collection of bugs that he has collected and mounted himself… he even has small boxes of spare parts, in case a bug is missing a leg, wing, etc.

Living in a large trailer home located somewhere in Wisconsin, visiting Mike is an adventure in itself. The décor of Mike's living space is decidedly retro, with stylishly chic 50/ 60s furnishings, odd figures and statues and, enough books and clippings to fill a warehouse, with a variety of sketches, drawings and reference photos

LEFT: 'Little Bad Wolf Meets Big Red Riding Hood'. BELOW: 'Sexy Sycra'. The bulk of Mike's art is monochrome, densely rendered in pencil.

tacked to the walls. The wall decorations also include two gigantic collages that Mike has been working on for many years—one devoted to Science-Fiction imagery and the other devoted to the nude female. Each collage consists of 1000s of meticulously cut out images.

If the serried ranks of 'bugmen', the piles of books and the collages aren't enough of a sensory assault, Mike has also, from time to time, exhibited a passion for exotic pets. As Ron tells it, "he has had pet snakes, tarantulas, and giant scorpions, that he will handle, and let climb up his arms…and dead mice in his freezer (food for pets)".

Mike's other big passion is the female foot. Insteps and arches, tendons and toes are all grist to Mike's mill. Over the years he has dedicated himself to this cause with

   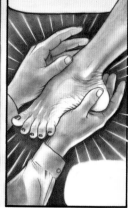

Covers and interior art from the ill-fated 'Untamed Foot Fantasy Romance'. Many years before the advent of crowd-funding sites, Mike set about creating his ultimate graphic novel. Sadly, no distributor would touch the comic and it has yet to see the light of day.

admirable zeal. His drawings ooze foot-fuelled fantasy, and the women he depicts eye their surroundings with an icy hauteur. Such is his dedication to the cause of advancing the appreciation of the female foot that in 2005 he produced and published a comic titled, *Untamed Foot Fantasy Romance*. Predictably no distributor was prepared to handle this "niche-market" gem and Mike still has piles of the comic competing for space with all the other antiquarian treasures that he has amassed over the years.

Mike has managed to keep just about every drawing that he has produced: much of his work is carefully archived in ring binders, and leafing through them is a delight for all connoisseurs of exotic insect life, well heeled dominatrices and worlds beyond our ken. His art is most frequently executed in pencil: his eye for detail and love of tone seem to be most suited to this medium.

Having had the privilege of viewing a small percentage of Mike's astonishing output, we can only hope that this feature will generate more well-deserved attention for his exquisite and captivating off-the-wall art.●

90

COMING SOON!!! *THE ULTIMATE GUIDE TO THE SPANISH ARTISTS WHOSE WORK CREATED A COMICS REVOLUTION —144 PAGES!*

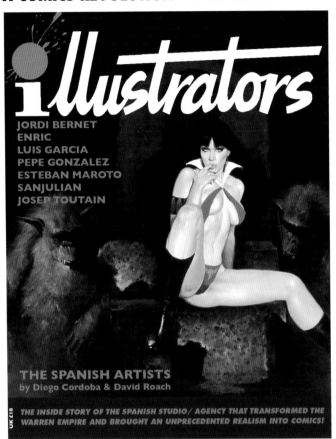

illustrators

JORDI BERNET
ENRIC
LUIS GARCIA
PEPE GONZALEZ
ESTEBAN MAROTO
SANJULIAN
JOSEP TOUTAIN

THE SPANISH ARTISTS
by Diego Cordoba & David Roach

UK £18

THE INSIDE STORY OF THE SPANISH STUDIO/ AGENCY THAT TRANSFORMED THE WARREN EMPIRE AND BROUGHT AN UNPRECEDENTED REALISM INTO COMICS!

Pepe Gonzalez

Sanjulian

Esteban Maroto

Enric

Luis Garcia

Jordi Bernet

Mermaid

The first in a series of breathtaking Giclee prints by award winning illustrator **Peter Richardson**. Measuring 8.5 x 23.5 inchs and printed on Somerset watercolor paper, this edition is strictly limited to 100 copies and comes hand signed and numbered with an accompanying certificate of authenticity.

UK £35, we also ship internationally—payment via PayPal.

peter-richardson-illustration.com

The Gallery: Fortunino Matania—the Art of Reportage Illustration

THE ART OF FORTUNINO MATANIA provided readers with an insight into news events that would otherwise have been impossible to document visually in an era when photography was still in its infancy.

His illustrations brought to life events which would have otherwise been beyond the comprehension of his audience. The sinking of the Titanic, the coronation of King Edward VII and his documentation of the First World War, present the viewer with images of astonishing vitality. His depictions of scenes from many periods of history were popular for much of the last century.

A new and sumptuous collection of his art is currently in development; titled 'The Art of Fortunino Matania—Drawing From History'. It is due for publication later this year by **Book Palace Books**.●

● *For more information about this and other similar projects—visit:* ***www.bookpalace.com.***

ABOVE: Matania documented the progress of the First World War from its commencement in August 1914 until the Armistice celebrations in November 1918. Often visiting the Front and interviewing hopsitalised survivors, his illustrations were based on solid research. Although occasionally prone to straying into the realms of romanticism, his work remains a powerful insight into the War.

WHITEBOX COLLECTABLES

comics • artbooks • original artwork • memorabilia

All Rights Reserved. Characters © DC Comics

With more than 40 years of collecting history, Whitebox Collectables is where it's at when it comes not only to original artwork and the four-colour thrills'n'spills of pre-Code comicbooks and 21st Century graphic novels but also the monochrome madness that graced the lobbies and billboards of movie houses of the 1950's... much of it discontinued and often signed!

WE ARE SPECIALISTS IN

- Golden & Silver-Age Comics
- Artbooks
- Movie Posters
- Graphic Novels
- Trade Paperbacks
- Film Memorabilia
- Original Artwork
- New Artbooks

WE BUY COMICS
ARE YOU SELLING YOUR COMIC COLLECTION?

...AND MUCH MORE!

VISIT OUR WEBSTORE AT:

www.whiteboxcollectables.co.uk

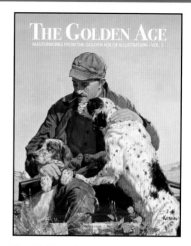

The Art of José Gonzalez
By David Roach
Foreword by Joe Jusko
Hardcover 268 pages
Dynamite £25.00/ $39.99

Paperback Parade # 89
Edited by Gary Lovisi
Softbound 104 pages
www.gryphonbooks.com
Gryphon Books $15.00

The Golden Age
Volume 3
Edited by Dan Zimmer
Hardbound 224 pages
The Illustrated Press $44.95

VAMPIRELLA IS ONE of the most iconic figures in the horror genre, at once both vampire and beautiful woman, but it was in the hands of Spanish artist José Gonzalez that she transcended the comic book boundaries and saved a company from bankruptcy. Though not created by Gonzalez (known as 'Pepe' by his colleagues and friends), he was the artist who best defined her.

At long last, *Dynamite* devotes a whole book to this rather erratic artist. Although considered 'lazy' by many in the profession, Pepe managed to produce quite a large selection of comic pages and illustrations during his lifetime, and this book easily attests to it. Favouring pencil and ink over other mediums, Pepe was certainly one of the top artists when it came to drawing beautiful girls. Here we get to see how he worked on different genres; westerns and romantic fiction for the British; horror stories for the Americans; erotic strips for the Spanish; move-star illustrations and covers for romance books around the world.

Crammed with reproductions of his work, including many examples scanned from original art, this is a must for fans of 'good-girl' art and *Vampirella*.

FOR READERS AND COLLECTORS of 'hard-boiled' paperbacks, there is no better resource than Gary Lovisi's *Paperback Parade*. Packed with features dedicated to the lurid world of paperback collecting (sleaze, sci-fi, horror, fantasy and oodles of 'good girl' abound) each issue punches well above its weight in terms of satisfying the needs of the connoisseur.

Paperback Parade knows how to appeal to its readership. Its authoritative and enlightening features are enlivened with colour reproductions of covers of variable merit, the works of Reginald Heade and Robert McGinnis rubbing shoulders with more pedestrian fare. For lovers of illustration, there is much to commend this publication, and Gary and his team often source samples of original artwork to display alongside the covers that appear on every page.

There are also moments of unalloyed 'nerdism', such as a feature showing a succession of 'swipes' taken from a cover by Rudy Nappi. A lot of these informative nuggets are provided by the readership, which greatly adds to the fun of the occasion.

Now in its 31st year of publication, this is an essential read for lovers of paperbacks and crime fiction.

THE THIRD VOLUME in this excellent series continues the tradition of Dan Zimmer's presentation of illustration which might otherwise be consigned to the realm of obscurity.

Published by Dan's *Illustrated Press*, these books present a great selection of illustrations that haven't, as yet, found a home within his other publishing activities—be that the pages of his long-running quarterly journal *Illustration* or any of the superb monographs of illustrators that he has published over the preceding years.

In this book, we are again treated to deliciously vibrant scans of original artwork encompassing a variety of genres, from Willy Pogany's satyrs, through Joseph Leyendecker's paint-sculpted witch on a broomstick, through to Robert McGinnis' tartan-robed and smoky-eyed seductress.

However, while it is great to see the work of famiiar names brought to life with such superb reproductions, it is often the work of the hitherto unfamiliar artists that makes one pause when leafing through these pages.

For lovers of great art and great illustration, this is a really delightful and rewarding book.

● Buy from ***www.bookpalace.com***

illustrators

artist index

BACK ISSUES!

Issue 1: Denis McLoughlin, Ian Kennedy, Badia Camps, Cheri Herouard, Mick Brownfield

Issue 2: David Wright, C.L. Doughty, Raymond Sheppard, Renato Fratini, Jordi Penalva

Issue 3: Fortunino Matania, Bernie Fuchs, Andy Virgil, Peter Maddocks, Micron Publishing,

Issue 4: Mike Johnson, Chris McEwan, The Pan Book of Horror Stories, Leslie Ashwell Wood

Issue 5: Mick Brownfield, Brian Sanders, Derek Eyles, Anne & Janet Grahame Johnstone

Issue 6: Walter Wyles, Dave Gaskill, Graham Coton, Laurence Fish, The Illustrators Workshop

Issue 7: Alan Lee, John Vernon Lord, Bernie Fuchs, Leif Peng, Mark English

Issue 8: Les Edwards, Bart Forbes, Sidney Paget, John Haslam, Bernie Fuchs, Zelda Devon

Issue 9: Bruce Pennington, Miss Led, Eric Parker, Will Terry, Bryn Havord

Issue 10: William Stout, Cynthia Sheppard, Patrick Nicolle, Amit Tayal, Wu Chen, Frank C. Papé

Issue 11: Donato Giancola, Tomer Hanuka, James McConnell, Mike Terry, Freya Hartas, Jonathan Burton, Gustave Doré

Issue 12: Android Jones, Denis Zilber, Howard Chaykin, Sidney Sime, Arty Freeman, Philip Mendoza

Issue 13: Mitch O'Connell, Jeff Miracola, Septimus Scott, Brooke Boynton Hughes, Tor Upson

Issue 14: Tara McPherson, Joe Jusko, Maurice Leloir, Adam Stower, Mike Zagorski

BACK ISSUES £18 EACH POST FREE

While stocks last
4 issue subscription UK £49
4 issue subscription EU/ USA £66
4 issue subscription ROW £72
All subscribers will receive a FREE 4
issue digital copy worth over £15

bookpalace.com

Tel: 020 8768 0022 (+44 20 8768 0022)
e-mail: IQ@bookpalace.com

95

It is always really heartwarming when we receive feedback from the artists that we feature—the message below is from Pacha who was our number one contact when we were working on Android Jones' feature in issue 12:

I received my copy of **illustrators** magazine and it is BEAUTIFUL! The print quality is fantastic, and the layout looks great! Nice JOB!

Andrew has requested a pdf version of the article. This way we can save it in our archives. Plus we run everything in digital, so we would love to have a copy in this format.

Thank you very much!

—Pacha

We were also extremely stoked when the amazingly talented Denis Zilber posted these pictures on his Facebook page apropos of his feature in issue 12:

My humble work got featured in issue #12 of Illustrators magazine. Thank you so much Peter Richardson! It's an honor!

👍 Like   💬 Comment   ↪ Share

You, Louise Gardner, Arty Freeman, Jon Ander Azaola and 440 others like this.

3 shares

View 18 more comments

Dana Boadway Masson Awesome!! Congrats!!
Like · Reply · 👍 1 · December 21, 2015 at 12:51pm

Sourish Mitra great
Like · Reply · 👍 1 · December 21, 2015 at 1:08pm

Naseem Padamshi Amazing...CONGRATS!
Like · Reply · 👍 1 · December 21, 2015 at 1:12pm

Tamara Osadcha Gratuliere Denis!
See Translation
Like · Reply · 👍 1 · December 25, 2015 at 8:54am

And we were honoured to receive the following message from Curt Swan biographer Eddy Zeno:

To those involved in the making of this fine publication;

Thank you; issue eleven was beautiful. I especially liked the treatment given to the career of James McConnell. Very much looking forward to the full-length book to come.

Thank you again, and best wishes;

—Eddy Zeno

We were very pleased to receive the following review of issue 9 from G.F. Willmetts, editor at:
SFCrowsnest.org.uk
which is the go-to resource for science fiction fans with monthly hits in excess of 100.000

As soon as I saw the cover of *Illustrators* 9, I recognised the work of Bruce Pennington because it's the cover of 'Time, Space And Nathaniel' by Brian Aldiss. It's also one of the few times where I bought the book for the cover art but didn't care for the stories (four of them) inside. Said art also graced the great *Science Fiction Monthly* magazine from the 70s, too, and that's where I learnt who painted it. A large part of this magazine is devoted to Pennington's work and life story and even, after all this time, a few surprises. He was the first to paint the original *NEL* 'Dune' trilogy and the first two covers aren't typically his work which is a lot finer but I suspect deadlines played a part in it. Pennington admits in his later years, he's not keen on tight deadlines. His work is also in gouache, a designer watercolour, layers of ink and varnish, making it even more remarkable because of his use of colour and nothing blending together.

Breaking into the industry after art college, Pennington's break came from film poster work before being able to make the jump into book covers and becoming an in-demand artist, especially in our genre, covering not only SF but fantasy and horror. The variety of his book covers is breathtaking and if you've missed out on his work, then this magazine will put things into context. I suspect if you own SF books from the 70s-80s, then you will probably already have some in your collection, just not knowing who did them. He was the main cover artist in the UK for writers Brian Aldiss and Ray Bradbury, amongst others.

If you want something away from our genre, an examination of the art of Joanna Henly who has an eye for drawing women with pale shades is worth looking at and a demonstration that less can make it look better.

Just in case you think all the artists here are contemporary, lastly there is a look at the work of Eric R. Parker. If the name doesn't sound too familiar, then you need to remember the private detective *Sexton Blake*. Long before Blake became an ITV children's series starring Laurence Payne and Roger Foss in the 1960s-70s, Parker illustrated the series in *Union Jack* magazine. The article here covers and shows a variety of other work he also did. From what is described, Parker could map out a design in his head and have it drawn out very quickly without any necessity to change things. Very prolific and this made for a nice icing on the cake.

Although *illustrators* is an expensive quarterly magazine and this edition is a year old, it does step into our genre from time to time and it might pay you to see who they cover next. Looking at the paper quality and being squarebound, explains its high price. If you are after specific editions, you might find it easier buy directly off *The Book Palace* than through other sources in the UK and, in the USA, via Bud Plant.

—G.F. Willmetts

Coming Soon
Neal Adams!